OF MAIM AND CURE

A collection of poems

For 16-year-old me; thanks for never
giving up…

CONTENTS

SECRET

Summer nights bleed through my win-
dow,

It's 4 am as we are laughing,

Your voice is like a velvet robe,

Soft on my soul and calming.

Not a wink of sleep caught in my spar-
kling eyes,

You are the cause of my insomnia.

Years and lifetimes pass swimming by,

Our hearts filled with this euphoria.

We keep this love in text messages,

In late night calls,

In journal pages,

We keep this love hidden from darting
eyes,

We keep this love a secret as it ages.

It rips my heart open to see

A love so true and understanding,

A love that makes me alive with every
breathe,

A love that's so sacrificing.

I do not care about right or wrong,

I do not care about breaking,

I do not care if we would end someday,

As long as (tonight) our love is breath-
ing.

~ *6th March, 2022.*

" *Distance creates loud spaces,
intimacy leads to chaotic calm-
ness, of both have I drank the
sheer ambrosia*'

FADE AWAY

Hey, I just dropped by to say,

The magic of us really did fade away.

Didn't it? Or am I overthinking?

Swimming backup yet sinking.

I've been so much better, thanks for
letting me in,

But why did you have to shut yourself
in?

I am in the hallway, the corridors of
your mind,

You're on the other side of the door,

Cutting the ties that bind…

Bind us together as identical broken
souls.

We were both tending to our wounded
holes.

Or tell me, be honest, did I not suc-
ceed?

Did I not succeed to be the friend in
need?

Or was I burdening you, making you
carry,

An extra baggage, hollow and dreary?

Sorry, I won't bother you with my in-
cessant chatter,

All that matters is that you feel better;

Better with your yearlong friend,

Better without me, us having an end.

…I guess I sound unlike me but I cannot help…

Help but wonder which was the day,

That the magic of us faded away.

~ 15th May, 2021.

"We agree to let go, a business handshake and a pat on the back…But what about this bloody pile of love I have for you? What about this carnal urge to kiss you every day?

PENITENCE

I have never learned

And yet I know so much.

My soul has itched and yearned

For a soul like yours as such.

And yet I know I've been exploiting you,

I know I've been unfair to you,

I know, I know and yet I don't.

I know I'm yours and that's all I learned.

I have wronged you, sliced you,

Bled through your wrists.

Broken your bones,

Under the pressure of my weights.

Weights of endless dilemma,

Pried open your limbs.

"I didn't mean to hurt you"

That's all they say.

And I'm deciding if saying it is enough.

Or shall I own up to my crime,

Covered in broken hearts and grime?

But really, do you think about it?

Would I have ever done it?

If only I could rip my heart away

From a nightmare existing far away,

If only I could vanish in thin air,

If only he was never there...?

I hate that I care

For all the wrong people

At all the wrong times,

And the pain in my heart is so deafening

I'm almost out of rhymes,

It's so cold and lonely

I deserve it and more, if only.

I know I can never be forgiven,

Neither by you nor by me.

I'm afraid of even saying sorry,

Because all my vindications will only

Sound like lies and lies and lies.

But one thing we both know is true,

As I'm writhing in agony and rue,

That I have loved you

Through all the highs and blues,

And you have loved me

Through all my crimes and ill virtues.

I know love is not all that is,

To cool the gaping wound on your chest.

So here I cross mine and pour

My blood, my soul and my utter best,

To win back what I can't afford to lose;

My soulmate with whom I have been blest.

*" I'll be your light house, not
your anchor..."*

HEALING IS ITSELF

Since healing is never leisure to me,

Healing for me is a series

Of falling down, getting a bloody lip,

And kissing the darkness on his finger-
tips.

Healing was a struggle to me;

Passing days as I pass my dead visage,

Telling myself it's a numb pity,

Telling myself it must pass as I age.

And as I sure aged,

Faster than I was designed to be,

Maybe because I was told

The more numbness I faced,

the further it will run from me.

"Run from me old friend, for if you love me, you must leave me, hanging at the altar of death"

Since healing is never leisure to me,

I made sure it is for my kins.

Kins I never met, friends unknown to me.

Yet we've walked on the same fire and pins.

And for me to find the peace I sought,

I had to seek their with my menial ardour,

Telling them tales no one told me,

Telling them lucid poetry, of mottle
and pallor.

Healing for me is now redolent,

Watching them fall down,

Skinning their knee.

Getting back up in invincible adoles-
cence.

As if I am a blue print, their guiding
phantasy.

As if I found healing in curing them,

My battle scars adorning their effigy.

Maybe it has taken me too long

Figuring out how to fix myself,

Because healing people who are battle-
worn,

Is healing to me itself.

Healing is itself…

~ *4th March, 2021.*

*"…And I was never sure
whether you were the light
house or the storm"*

AND WE STAND AT DEATH

You're no longer the smile

I died to feel through my phone,

Nor are you the voice ringing through
my head.

All that's left is a spectre monotone;

A love that has been cudgelled to
death.

I refuse to be haunted by your bloody
face,

The moment I pulped it with my fal-
sity.

Rather I wish, to be possessed by your
kinder grace,

The love that you poured with generos-
ity.

I wish to unlearn, the pattern of devo-
tion

To which your leftover history is
clamped.

Suffocating me with undead emotions,

Unsaid truths kept crushed and
cramped.

I remember every word that spilled
from that mouth so tame.

I remember every note of your laugh,

For god's sake, I even remember your
bike's name,

And I remember trusting all that bluff.

Heart don't break easily,

Hearts don't have bones.

Yet I think I grew one for you

That fractures and aches and moans.

~ *21st May, 2022.*

" One day, when we'll drift apart, torn from the limbs, oceans to continents, we would haunt each other, We'll walk away, pieces of each other in hand, threatening to turn to dust, we'll never look back as we promised…and yet when we rip these strings apart, we bleed each other's blood."

YOU ARE BOTH

You are my glory, and you, my shame.

The unspoken sighs in my name.

A breathless kiss,

A soundless shriek,

The breeze of love and the flame of the
same.

You are my secret, and the loudest
truth ever spoken.

So fragile in my arms and yet not bro-
ken,

I wonder how I'd have been,

Neither happier nor green.

If I don't feel your presence, shall I
never awaken.

You are my best friend and you my
lover,

A notorious bond painted with ro-
mance's colour.

A touchless hug,

An intimate laugh,

The bloodiest wound from which

I can never recover.

My anger and my respite, you are the
source,

Changing my mood like a river its
changing course.

Building and breaking,

Meandering and turning,

My beacon of all colours, brightness at
full force.

Rarely a settler, and always a traveller;

You're an adventurer, a splendid story-
teller.

Quivering paranoia,

Of losing you forever.

We're always at poles and yet so similar.

You're my confusion; an itching query.

Lately you have been

The sole occupant of my diary.

Your warm brown eyes,

Your joyful smiles.

My flawless perfection, whom I love
sincerely.

Riskiest loss and most lucrative gain,

You are my pleasure and you my pain.

I breathe in your inflictions,

Merely as love,

One can only do that, and never complain.

Softest touch in burning agony;

I fail to remember them all too many,

Am I hurt?

Or just drunk in affection?

I wonder in the blinding epiphany.

A hopeful dawn but the duskiest twilight,

Every time we're together, and when I lose your sight.

Deepest regret I cannot undo,

Deepest love I can't render untrue;

Not in a million years have I been in such plight.

Every rhyme I envisage, you are the thought behind it

Every word that is born in me, you are the sire of it.

If writing was a nuptial bond, honey we are already fastened.

We are only moving so fast because our destiny was hastened.

If poetry was a sin, darling we are criminals in endeavour.

You are both,

My life and demise,

You are my never and forever.

~ 16th April, 2022.

*" Everybody has a secret world
inside them…you were mine,"*

TIME MACHINE

Time machine,

Save my life from these memories.

For I feel like I'm frozen in time,

Like I never was seventeen.

Plaid green skirts,

Redone braids and friendly flirts,

Never knew it would become a love

One that knows how to scar and hurt.

And I wish it ended right there,

One sided love, none to compare.

But she had to break free,

Take all parts of me

And freeze in this moment right here.

Inside jokes,

Hour long calls and abusive folks,

Walked through hell and burned to-
gether,

We had so many dreams and hopes.

And I wish I could be with her there,

As she glitched through the world so
unfair ,

But I had to annihilate,

Every moment we had made,

And freeze their corpses right here.

~ 12th June, 2022.

" I am typing out a reply to you when I hear her, ' It hurts, it hurts, it hurts'. I ignore and think, ' When does it not?' "

JOHNATHAN

December night, our paths collided.

The strangest scene ever seen;

Hunting for the author to your favour-
ite book,

I guess you can say my words lured you
in.

Time flew by one fine spring morning,

My heart heavy in despair,

You swung in like the vampire you are,

Telling me at least somebody cares.

You forgave me for being hard on my-
self,

You understood what's unspeakable,

You shook me out of my myths,

And made me realize love's not a fair-
ytale or a fable.

Love, in fact, is overrated,

What matters is what makes us glad.

Someone who accepts me flawed and
fallen,

Happy, broken or sad.

When pages of my life started fading
away

You drowned me in your colour,

When winters started bleeding in me,

You kissed me with your summer.

It's scary how wrong everything feels,

How unbelievably close each day we
grow,

But we aren't moving too fast honey,

We're just burning bright and slow.

We don't have to rush anything,

We don't have to call it a day,

Even though we are John and Lily,

We don't only have one today.

I'm not scared of being wrong any-
more,

Like I used to be a few days ago,

All I care is to fly high with you,

The world judging me below.

*~ 5th **March, 2022.***

"Without pain we are all just shapeless bundles of joy; bliss-fully ignorant"

INTERTWINED

What if I sleep and never wake up?

> *"I'd be there, to kiss open your eyes"*

What if I am late?

What if I miss the train?

> *"We can sleep in together with coffee mugs,*
>
> *Kitchen tops in the April rain"*

What if I don't stay the same?

> *"I'd rearrange my soul as well"*

What if I call?

> *"I'd always answer"*

What if I don't go?

> *"I'd let you stay"*

What if I fall?

> *"You know who you're going to land on"*

What if they show?

> *"I'd hide you in my bones"*

Among all the anxious moments one
thing is the same,

My love for you is to blame.

> *"And no one blames you ever my love,*
>
> *For you I'm half-crazy myself"*

And just in case nobody told you this,

The way you are holding up with all the
mess,

I'm proud of you my dearest.

"And I of you my moon, for loving a mess so intertwined.

For being so brave so as to love a sinner who never truly learned how to belong to one person alone.

Penitent and yet, not guilty as much is she,

Because being such a mess has brought her to you, what else can she ask for?"

~ 12th April, 2022.

*"Somebody, something be-
tween us was dying.*

*Only I felt parts of me being
pulled into the grave."*

A BOOK MISJUDGED

I am an open book, infringe me as you like.

Hide me from the world, chain me with spikes.

For I am a slave to you, my God, my muse,

Translate my gibberish, tarnished and confused.

Misjudged and misunderstood

Are the coils of my mind since childhood.

Help me release them into kites,

Annotate my mind as you like.

Mark the chapters that you love to
read,

Mark my skin with every desired deed,

If you cannot get enough,

Break my spine,

Undo those pages,

Unravel me thine.

I'm an open book and fiction is my be-
lief,

Living in a fairytale is my only sense of
relief.

If poetry is my prayer then you my
God,

Have the power to unleash me with
your sword.

I'm chained in the chains of love,

I'm chained as though a restless dove.

I'm tethered to you by the tip of my
quill,

I'm tethered to you against my will.

How do I stop worshipping you with
every word I write?

How do I see you as just a friend with
every urge I fight?

"I'm an open book" I echo as I close,

Bracing my shaken arms,

Needing myself the most.

~ 9th June, 2022.

Acknowledgement

The existence of this book is an absolute dream come true. A few years ago, I wouldn't even dare to think of putting my work out there so vulnerably, to be viewed by the world. My low self-esteem wouldn't be able to handle it. But now, thanks to some amazing people in my life, their appreciation and guidance, and incessant support has empowered me to finally embody the purpose of my life. I've grown and learnt a lot as I have fell and got up and I'm grateful for their contribution in my life.

I'd like to thank my family and my loved one, for supporting me and

letting me pursue my interests. My
friends for being honestly critical and
equally appreciative of my work and
providing proper guidance. Thanks for
helping with the entire process of pub-
lishing this book.

And lastly my muses, without whom
none of these words would have been
born in me.

About The Author

Abhilasha Parui is a promising writer and a young university student hailing from Kolkata, India who is currently pursuing her Bachelor's degree in English with Honours. With a natural gift of words, her poetry explores personal accounts of growth, love and the general ups and downs of life, often delving into confessional themes. She is also known as the author of her debut collection, **"Of Maim And Cure: a collection of poems"**.

Share your thoughts about her book with her on social media or via email.

✉ abhilashaparuiofficial@gmail.com

@abhilashaparui